HOLT
1
SPANISH

¡Ven conmigo!®

Alternative Assessment Guide

HOLT, RINEHART AND WINSTON

A Harcourt Classroom Education Company

Austin · New York · Orlando · Atlanta · San Francisco · Boston · Dallas · Toronto · London

Contributing Writer:

Catherine Dallas Purdy

Reviewers:

Richard Lindley
Mayanne Wright

Cover Photo/Illustration Credits: Group of students: Marty Granger/HRW Photo; project supplies: Sam Dudgeon/HRW Photo

¡VEN CONMIGO! is a trademark licensed to Holt, Rinehart and Winston, registered in the United States of America and/or other jurisdictions.

Printed in the United States of America

ISBN 0-03-065536-6

1 2 3 4 5 6 7   066   05 04 03 02 01

Contents

To the Teacher

Individual students have individual needs and ways of learning and progress at different rates in the development of their oral and written skills. The *Alternative Assessment Guide* is designed to accommodate those differences, and to offer opportunities for all students to be evaluated in the most favorable light possible and under circumstances that enable them to succeed.

The *Alternative Assessment Guide* contains information and suggestions for assessing student progress in three ways that go beyond the standard quizzes and tests: portfolio assessment, performance assessment, and CD-ROM Assessment. Each section of the guide contains some general information and specific, chapter-related suggestions for incorporating each type of assessment into your instructional plan.

Portfolio Assessment

Student portfolios are of great benefit to foreign language students and teachers alike because they provide documentation of a student's efforts, progress, and achievements over a given period of time. In addition, students can receive both positive feedback and constructive criticism by sharing their portfolios with teachers, family, and peers. The opportunity for self-reflection provided by using a portfolio encourages students to participate in their learning in a positive way, thus fostering pride, ownership, and self-esteem.

This guide includes a variety of materials that will help you implement and assess student portfolios. The written and oral activity evaluation forms, student and teacher checklists, peer editing rubric, and portfolio evaluation sheets included here are designed for use with student portfolios, or for independent use as part of any assessment program.

Determining a Purpose

The first step in implementing portfolios in your classroom is to determine the purpose for which they will be used. You can use portfolios to assess individual students' growth and progress, to make students active in the assessment process, to provide evidence and documentation of students' work for more effective communication with parents, or to evaluate an instructional program of curriculum. Both the contents of the portfolio and the manner in which it is to be evaluated will depend directly on the purpose(s) the portfolio is to serve. Before including any work in their portfolios, students should understand the purpose of the portfolio and the criteria by which their work will be evaluated.

Setting up the Portfolios

While portfolios can be used to meet a variety of objectives, they are especially useful tools for assessing written and oral work. Written items can be in a variety of formats including lists, posters, personal correspondence, poems, stories, articles, and essays, depending on the level and needs of the students. Oral items, such as conversations, interviews, commercials, and skits, may be recorded on audio- or videocassette for incorporation into the portfolio. Whatever the format, both written and oral work can include evidence of the developmental process, such as notes from brainstorming, outlines, early drafts, or scripts, as well as the finished product.

Each student can be responsible for keeping the materials selected for his or her portfolio. Encourage students to personalize the presentation of their portfolios and to keep in mind that their portfolios may include audiocassettes, videocassettes, or diskettes, as well as papers.

Selecting Materials for the Portfolio

There are several ways you and your students can select materials to include in portfolios. The portfolio should not be seen as a repository for all student work. Work to be included should be selected on the basis of the portfolio's purpose and evaluation criteria to be used.

Student Selection Many teachers prefer to let students choose samples of their best work to include in their portfolios. Early in the year, you may tell students how many written and oral items to include in their portfolios (for example, one written item and one oral item per chapter) and allow students the freedom to choose those pieces that they feel best represent their ability in the language. In this case, the written and oral portfolio items suggested in this guide would be treated as any other writing or speaking activities, and students would have the option to include these in their portfolios. This option empowers students by allowing them to decide what to include in their portfolios. The feeling of ownership of the portfolio is likely to increase as their involvement at the decision-making level increases.

Teacher-Directed Selection Some teachers prefer to maintain portfolios that contain students' responses to specific prompts or activities. The oral and written portfolio items suggested in this guide, or other writing or speaking activities of the teacher's choice, could be assigned specifically for inclusion in the portfolio. This type of portfolio allows the teacher to focus attention on specific functions, vocabulary items, and grammar points.

Collaborative Selection A third option is some combination of the two approaches described above. You can assign specific activities from which students may choose what to include in their portfolios, or you can assign some specific activities and allow students to choose others on their own. The collaborative approach allows you to focus on specific objectives, while at the same time giving students the opportunity to showcase what they feel is their best work.

As the classroom teacher, you are in the best position to decide what type of portfolio is most beneficial for your program and students. The most important step is to decide what objectives and outcomes the portfolio should assess, and then assign or help students select items that will best reflect those objectives and outcomes.

Chapter-Specific Portfolio Suggestions

Specific portfolio suggestions, one written and one oral, are provided for each chapter. These suggestions are based on existing *Pupil's Edition* activities that have been expanded to incorporate most of the functions and the vocabulary for each chapter. These materials may be included in the students' portfolios or used as guidelines for the inclusion of other materials.

Using the Portfolio Checklists

The checklists on pages 14 and 15 will help you and your students keep their portfolios organized. The *Student's Portfolio Checklist* is designed to help students track the items they include. The *Teacher's Portfolio Checklist* is a list of the items you expect students to include. If you choose to allow students to select materials for their portfolios, your checklist will be very general, specifying only the types of items and the dates on which each item should be included. Your checklist will be more specific if you are assigning specific portfolio activities, as it should indicate the particular activities you have assigned and the dates on which they are to be included.

Peer Editing

Peer editing provides students an opportunity to help each other develop writing skills. It also promotes an atmosphere of responsibility and teamwork through the writing process. We have included a *Peer Editing Rubric* to encourage peer editing in the classroom, and to aid students in this part of the evaluation process. Using the rubric, students can exchange compositions (usually a first draft), and edit each other's work according to a clearly designed, step-by-step process. The rubric is divided into three parts. Part I helps students examine the overall content of the written assignment using specific question prompts concerning vocabulary, organization, detail, and description. Part II helps students examine grammar and mechanics. In this part, teachers can tailor the goal of the assignment by outlining for the students the specific functions and grammar on which their editing should focus. For example, in Chapter 3, you might choose to focus on adjective agreement, or, in Chapter 4, you might choose functions for talking about free time. Use the space labeled "Target Functions and Grammar" in the *Peer Editing Rubric* for this purpose. Part III asks students to discuss the first two parts of the rubric in an effort to have them evaluate each other's work critically. Even though the rubric is organized in a step-by-step manner, your help in addressing students' questions will further increase the effectiveness of the peer editing process. The *Peer Editing Rubric* can be used with any written assignment.

Documenting Group Work

Very often a group-work project cannot be included in an individual's portfolio because of its size or the difficulties involved in making copies for each group member (posters, bulletin boards, videos, and so on). Other group or pair activities, such as conversations or skits, cannot be included in the portfolio unless they are recorded. To help students document such activities in their portfolios, you may want to use the *Documentation of Group Work* form on page 13.

Evaluating the Total Portfolio

Exactly how and how often you evaluate your students' complete portfolios will depend on the stated purpose. Ideally, students' portfolios should be evaluated at regular intervals over the course of the academic year. You should establish the length of the assessment period in advance—six weeks, a quarter, a semester, and so on. The *Portfolio Self-Evaluation* and *Portfolio Evaluation* forms on pages 16–17 are designed to aid you and your students in assessing the portfolio at the end of each assessment period. In order to ensure that portfolios are progressing successfully, you might want to meet individually with each student throughout each assessment period. In addition, individual conferences with students should be scheduled at the end of each evaluation period to discuss their portfolios and compare your assessement with their own.

Performance Assessment

Performance assessment provides an alternative to traditional testing methods by using authentic situations as contexts for performing communicative, competency-based tasks. For every chapter of the *Pupil's Edition*, this guide provides performance assessment suggestions to go with each **paso** of the chapter and one suggestion for global performance assessment that involves vocabulary and functions from the entire chapter. These suggestions give students the opportunity to demonstrate both acquired language proficiency and cultural competence in interviews, conversations, dialogues, or skits that can be performed for the entire class, or recorded or videotaped for evaluation at a later time. Performance assessment recordings can be included in student portfolios, or used independently, according to your needs for oral evaluation.

Using CD-ROM for Assessment

The *¡Ven conmigo! Interactive CD-ROM Program* provides a unique tool for evaluating students' language proficiency and for incorporating technology in the classroom. CD-ROM technology appeals to a variety of student learning styles, and offers you an efficient means by which to gauge student progress. This guide provides instructions for written activities, such as lists, letters, e-mail, journal entries, and advertisements. Oral activities include conversations, interviews, and dialogues. Writing and recording features also enable you to create your own activities and to evaluate student work according to your particular needs. Student work can be saved to a disk and included in students' portfolios.

Rubrics and
Evaluation Guidelines

Oral Rubric A

Use the following criteria to evaluate oral assignments. For assignments where comprehension is difficult to evaluate, you might want to give students full credit for comprehension or weigh other categories more heavily.

	4	3	2	1
Content	**Complete**	**Generally complete**	**Somewhat complete**	**Incomplete**
	Speaker consistently uses the appropriate functions and vocabulary necessary to communicate.	Speaker usually uses the appropriate functions and vocabulary necessary to communicate.	Speaker sometimes uses the appropriate functions and vocabulary necessary to communicate.	Speaker uses few of the appropriate functions and vocabulary necessary to communicate.
Comprehension	**Total comprehension**	**General comprehension**	**Moderate comprehension**	**Little comprehension**
	Speaker understands all of what is said to him or her.	Speaker understands most of what is said to him or her.	Speaker understands some of what is said to him or her.	Speaker understands little of what is said to him or her.
Comprehensibility	**Comprehensible**	**Usually comprehensible**	**Sometimes comprehensible**	**Seldom comprehensible**
	Listener understands all of what the speaker is trying to communicate.	Listener understands most of what the speaker is trying to communicate.	Listener understands less than half of what the speaker is trying to communicate.	Listener understands little of what the speaker is trying to communicate.
Accuracy	**Accurate**	**Usually accurate**	**Sometimes accurate**	**Seldom accurate**
	Speaker uses language correctly including grammar, spelling, word order, and punctuation.	Speaker usually uses language correctly including grammar, spelling, word order, and punctuation.	Speaker has some problems with language usage.	Speaker makes many errors in language usage.
Fluency	**Fluent**	**Moderately fluent**	**Somewhat fluent**	**Not fluent**
	Speaker speaks clearly without hesitation. Pronunciation and intonation sound natural.	Speaker has few problems with hesitation, pronunciation, and/or intonation.	Speaker has some problems with hesitation, pronunciation, and/or intonation.	Speaker hesitates frequently and struggles with pronunciation and intonation.

Nombre _____ Clase _____ Fecha _____

Oral Rubric B

Assignment _____

Targeted function(s) _____

_____

Targeted vocabulary _____

Targeted grammar _____

Content	You used the functions and vocabulary necessary to communicate.	(Excellent)	4	3	2	1	(Poor)
Comprehension	You understood what was said to you and responded appropriately.	(Excellent)	4	3	2	1	(Poor)
Comprehensibility	The listener was able to understand what you were trying to communicate.	(Excellent)	4	3	2	1	(Poor)
Accuracy	You used language correctly including grammar, spelling, word order, and punctuation.	(Excellent)	4	3	2	1	(Poor)
Fluency	You spoke clearly and without hesitation. Your pronunciation and intonation sounded natural.	(Excellent)	4	3	2	1	(Poor)

Total Score _____

Comments _____

_____

_____

_____

Nombre _____ Clase _____ Fecha _____

 Oral Progress Report

OVERALL IMPRESSION

☐ Excellent   ☐ Good   ☐ Satisfactory   ☐ Unsatisfactory

Some aspects of this item that are particularly good are _____

_____

_____

_____

_____

Some areas that could be improved are _____

_____

_____

_____

_____

To improve your speaking, I recommend _____

_____

_____

_____

_____

Additional Comments _____

_____

_____

_____

_____

Written Rubric A

Use the following criteria to evaluate written assignments.

	4	**3**	**2**	**1**
Content	Complete	Generally complete	Somewhat complete	Incomplete
	Writer uses the appropriate functions and vocabulary for the topic.	Writer usually uses the appropriate functions and vocabulary for the topic.	Writer uses few of the appropriate functions and vocabulary for the topic.	Writer uses none of the appropriate functions and vocabulary for the topic.
Comprehensibility	Comprehensible	Usually comprehensible	Sometimes comprehensible	Seldom comprehensible
	Reader can understand all of what the writer is trying to communicate.	Reader can understand most of what the writer is trying to communicate.	Reader can understand less than half of what the writer is trying to communicate.	Reader can understand little of what the writer is trying to communicate.
Accuracy	Accurate	Usually accurate	Sometimes accurate	Seldom accurate
	Writer uses grammar, spelling, word order, and punctuation correctly.	Writer usually uses grammar, vocabulary, and functions correctly.	Writer has some problems with language usage.	Writer makes a significant number of errors in language usage.
Organization	Well-organized	Generally well-organized	Somewhat organized	Poorly organized
	Presentation is logical and effective.	Presentation is generally logical and effective with a few minor problems.	Presentation is somewhat illogical and confusing in places.	Presentation lacks logical order and organization.
Effort	Excellent effort	Good effort	Moderate effort	Minimal effort
	Writer exceeds the requirements of the assignment and has put care and effort into the process.	Writer fulfills all of the requirements of the assignment.	Writer fulfills some of the requirements of the assignment.	Writer fulfills few of the requirements of the assignment.

¡Ven conmigo! Level 1

Nombre _____ Clase _____ Fecha _____

 Written Rubric B

Assignment _____

Targeted function(s) _____

_____

Targeted vocabulary _____

Targeted grammar _____

Content	You used the functions and vocabulary necessary to communicate.	(Excellent)	4	3	2	1	(Poor)
Comprehensibility	The reader was able to understand what you were trying to communicate.	(Excellent)	4	3	2	1	(Poor)
Accuracy	You used grammar, spelling, word order, and punctuation correctly.	(Excellent)	4	3	2	1	(Poor)
Organization	Your presentation was logical and effective.	(Excellent)	4	3	2	1	(Poor)
Effort	You put a lot of thought and effort into this assignment.	(Excellent)	4	3	2	1	(Poor)

Total Score _____

Comments _____

_____

_____

_____

¡Ven conmigo! Level 1

Alternative Assessment Guide **7**

Written Progress Report

OVERALL IMPRESSION

☐ Excellent   ☐ Good   ☐ Satisfactory   ☐ Unsatisfactory

Some aspects of this item that are particularly good are _____

_____

_____

_____

_____

Some areas that could be improved are _____

_____

_____

_____

_____

To improve your written work, I recommend _____

_____

_____

_____

_____

Additional Comments _____

_____

_____

_____

_____

_____

Peer Editing Rubric

Chapter _____

I. **Content:** Look for the following elements in your partner's composition. Put a check next to each category when you finish it.

1. _____ Vocabulary — Does the composition use enough new vocabulary from the chapter? Underline all the new vocabulary words you find from this chapter. What additional words do you suggest that your partner try to use?

2. _____ Organization — Is the composition organized and easy to follow? Can you find an introduction and a conclusion?

3. _____ Comprehensibility — Is the composition clear and easy to understand? Is there a specific part that was hard to understand? Did you understand the author's meaning? Draw a box around any sections that were particularly hard to understand.

4. _____ Target Functions and Grammar — Ask your teacher what functions and grammar you should focus on for this chapter and list them below.

Focus: _____

II. **Proofreader's checklist:** Circle any errors you find in your partner's composition. See the chart for some examples.

incorrect form of the verb	Yo (coma) como una hamburguesa.
Adjective– noun agreement / Subject –Verb agreement	mi casa es (blanco). blanca / Las amigas son (inteligente). inteligentes / Los perros (es) son bonitos.
Spelling	Eres (intelligente). inteligente
Article	(El) La casa es bonita.
Transition words (if they apply to chapter)	primero, después, y, o, por eso...
Accents/Punctuation	Buenos (dias) días / ¡Qué bueno ()!

III. Explain your content and grammar suggestions to your partner. Answer any questions about the edits.

Peer Editor's signature: _____ Date: _____

Portfolio Suggestions

Documentation of Group Work

Item _____ Chapter _____

Group Members: _____

_____

_____

_____

_____

_____

_____

Description of Item: _____

_____

_____

_____

_____

_____

_____

Personal Contribution: _____

_____

_____

_____

_____

_____

_____

Please rate your personal contribution to the group's work.

☐ Excellent   ☐ Good   ☐ Satisfactory   ☐ Unsatisfactory

Nombre _____ Clase _____ Fecha _____

Student's Portfolio Checklist

To the Student This form should be used to keep track of the materials you are including in your portfolio. It is important that you keep this list up to date so that your portfolio will be complete at the end of the assessment period. As you build your portfolio, try to include pieces of your work that demonstrate progress in your ability to speak and write in Spanish.

	Type of Item	Date Completed	Date Placed in Portfolio
Item #1			
Item #2			
Item #3			
Item #4			
Item #5			
Item #6			
Item #7			
Item #8			
Item #9			
Item #10			
Item #11			
Item #12			

¡Ven conmigo! Level 1

Nombre _____ Clase _____ Fecha _____

 Teacher's Portfolio Checklist

To the Teacher This form should be used to keep track of the materials you expect your students to keep in their portfolios for the semester. Encourage students to keep their lists up-to-date so that their portfolios will be complete at the end of the assessment period.

	Type of Item	Date Assigned	Date Due in Portfolio
Item #1			
Item #2			
Item #3			
Item #4			
Item #5			
Item #6			
Item #7			
Item #8			
Item #9			
Item #10			
Item #11			
Item #12			

Nombre _____ Clase _____ Fecha _____

 Portfolio Self-Evaluation

To the Student Your portfolio consists of selections of your written and oral work. You should consider all the items in your portfolio as you evaluate your progress. Read the statements below and mark a box to the right of each statement that shows how well your portfolio demonstrates your skills and abilities in Spanish.

	Strongly Agree	Agree	Disagree	Strongly Disagree
1. My portfolio contains all of the required items.				
2. My portfolio provides evidence of my progress in speaking and writing Spanish.				
3. The items in my portfolio demonstrate that I can communicate my ideas in Spanish.				
4. The items in my portfolio demonstrate accurate use of Spanish.				
5. The items in my portfolio show that I understand and can use a wide variety of vocabulary.				
6. When creating the items in my portfolio, I tried to use what I have learned in new ways.				
7. The items in my portfolio provide an accurate picture of my skills and abilities in Spanish.				

My favorite item in my portfolio is _____

because (please give at least three reasons) _____

_____

_____

_____

_____

_____

_____

_____

In assessing my overall portfolio, I find it to be (check one):

☐ Excellent   ☐ Good   ☐ Satisfactory   ☐ Unsatisfactory

¡Ven conmigo! Level 1

Portfolio Evaluation

To the Student   I have reviewed the items in your portfolio and want to share with you my reactions to your work.

Teacher's Signature _____

Date _____

	Strongly Agree	Agree	Disagree	Strongly Disagree
1. Your portfolio contains all of the required items.				
2. Your portfolio provides evidence of your progress in speaking and writing Spanish.				
3. The items in your portfolio demonstrate that you can communicate your ideas in Spanish.				
4. The items in your portfolio demonstrate accurate use of Spanish.				
5. The items in your portfolio demonstrate the use of a wide variety of Spanish vocabulary.				
6. When creating the items in your portfolio, you have tried to use what you have learned in new ways.				
7. The items in your portfolio provide an accurate picture of your skills and abilities in Spanish.				

My favorite item in your portfolio is _____

because _____

_____

_____

One area in which you seem to need improvement is _____

_____

For your next portfolio collection, I would like to suggest _____

_____

In assessing your overall portfolio, I find it to be (check one):

☐ Excellent   ☐ Good   ☐ Satisfactory   ☐ Unsatisfactory

¡Mucho gusto!

Written: Activity 36

Expanded Activity Students should imagine that they have met several Spanish-speaking exchange students who don't know English very well yet. They want to make a good impression and introduce their Spanish-speaking friends to the teacher in Spanish, telling their names, ages, and hometowns. Instruct students to write the necessary questions on an index card to get this information. They should then interview the other students and write the answers on their index cards.

Purpose to practice writing simple questions and answers in Spanish: introducing people and responding to an introduction; asking and saying how old someone is; asking where someone is from

Rationale Applying the targeted functional expressions to an authentic situation helps students recognize that they're learning language for communication. Writing these expressions in an authentic context also helps students to internalize the expressions.

Materials Each student will need a 3 x 5-inch index card and a pen.

Portfolio Item Students should put the index cards with interview questions and answers into their portfolios. Taping the index cards to an 8 1/2 x 11-inch piece of paper may make storage easier.

Oral: Repaso Activity 5

Expanded Activity Students will use the information they got in their interviews to make introductions at a party. Be sure students have memorized the information written on their cards, because they should not use the cards during the role-play. Move the classroom furniture to create a party area by arranging chairs around an empty space. Use the door of the classroom as the front door of the teacher's apartment. Some students are already at the party, and others are in the hall ready to arrive. Arriving at the party, the students exchange greetings and introduce the newcomers to their friends and to the teacher, telling each person's name, age, and hometown.

Purpose to practice making introductions: saying hello and goodbye; introducing people and responding to an introduction; asking and saying how old someone is; asking where someone is from and saying where you're from

Rationale Simulating real situations helps students activate the language and accelerates their learning.

Materials You will need audio or video equipment to record the activity and individual cassettes or a class master for incorporation into students' portfolios.

Portfolio Item Record students' greetings and introductions on audio- or videocassette for incorporation into their portfolios.

¡Organízate!

Written: Activity 35

Expanded Activity Have each student bring a photo of two or more people they know to class and use it to write some sentences about the people. They should tell who each person is, the person's age, and something he or she needs or wants for school or for his or her room at home. The finished product can be mounted on poster board or construction paper and posted in the classroom.

Purpose to practice talking about what people need and want and to review skills learned in **Capítulo 1**: introducing someone; saying how old someone is; talking about likes and dislikes; and talking about what someone wants and needs

Rationale Talking about people they know captures the students' interest. Writing something that everyone can read and discuss gives students another opportunity to use the new language and practice their newly acquired vocabulary.

Materials pen/pencil and paper; poster board or construction paper, glue stick

Portfolio Item Either the finished product or a photocopy of it can be placed in the student's portfolio.

Oral: A ver si puedo... Activity 2

Expanded Activity Have students work with partners. Each pair creates a description of an ideal bedroom. Have them discuss together what things they want or need in the room. What do they NOT want or need? Are there things they agree on? When students have finished their description, record their conversation on video- or audiotape.

Purpose to practice describing the contents of one's room; to practice telling what you want or need; to practice listening and responding to a partner

Rationale Knowing the vocabulary and structures necessary to discuss one's personal space allows students to talk about something that is important to them.

Materials audio or video recording equipment

Portfolio Item recording of the conversation

Nuevas clases, nuevos amigos

Written: Repaso Activity 2

Expanded Activity Each student writes his or her class schedule, using a form, either written on the board or as a handout. The form should look like the class schedule on p. 104 and should include times, courses, and teachers. Have students imagine that they're comparing their schedules with that of a good friend. Have each student write a note to his or her friend, summarizing when the different classes meet.

Purpose to practice writing about schedules, talking about classes, sequencing events, and telling time

Rationale Discussing schedules and courses is an everyday skill that students will want to learn so that they can talk to each other about their daily lives.

Materials paper, pens, pencils, blank class schedules

Portfolio Item The written class schedule and the follow-up note can both be a part of the student's written portfolio.

Oral: Repaso Activity 3

Expanded Activity The oral activity is an extension of the written portfolio suggestion. Students exchange schedules with another student. They read their partner's schedule, and then talk with that person about what is in the schedule. They should find out why their partner is taking certain classes, which ones he or she likes or dislikes, and then see if they agree with their partner's likes and dislikes. Have them figure out if they and their partner are taking any of the same classes at the same time, if their opinions about these classes are the same, and if they have the same opinions about the teachers. Have them record their conversation.

Purpose to practice talking about class schedules and likes and dislikes: talking about class schedules, sequencing events, telling time, and things you like, and explaining why

Rationale Being able to communicate schedules and sequence events is essential as people juggle and coordinate all they have to do.

Material Students will need paper, pens or pencils, blank class schedules, audio or video equipment, and blank cassettes.

Portfolio Item Record the conversation on audio- or videocassette for incorporation into portfolios.

¿Qué haces esta tarde?

Written: Activity 32

Expanded Activity Have students ask their partners what activities they like or don't like to do during the following times: after class, during their free time, and on Saturdays. For example: **Después de la clase me gusta hablar por teléfono** or **Despúes de la clase no me gusta sacar la basura.** Students should mention two activities for each of the three categories. Partners will take notes and write a report about each other's likes and dislikes. Students should switch roles to allow each of them to gather the information for the report.

Purpose to practice taking notes and the present tense of regular verbs; to practice likes and dislikes

Rationale Gathering information and then writing about it is a general skill that students can use in other subject areas.

Materials No special materials needed.

Portfolio Item Students may include their original notes and the final report about their partner in their written portfolios.

Oral: Activity 30

Expanded Activity Have the entire class work together to create a list of ten days and times that would fall during free time. For example, one might say **los viernes a las cinco de la tarde.** Write the list on the board. Group the students into pairs. One student writes the first five times and days on five small pieces of paper. The other one writes the last five. The papers are folded and put into a hat. Pairs take turns drawing these numbers and asking a question with the day and time; for example, **¿Dónde estás los viernes a las cinco de la tarde?** The partner answers, **Estoy...,** telling where he or she usually is at that time. The partner who asks the question is the only one to see the paper. If the other partner doesn't understand, he or she needs to ask for clarification.

Purpose to practice asking and listening to questions and responding appropriately: discussing what you and others do during free time and talking about where you and others go during free time

Rationale Asking questions and responding appropriately are skills that need to be developed over a period of time and should be repeated frequently.

Materials pens, small pieces of paper, and something for a hat; audio or video recording equipment

Portfolio Item Students may want to record the conversation and place it in the oral portfolio.

5 El ritmo de la vida

Written: Activity 27

Expanded Activity Have students look for a weather map from Latin America. Students can use the weather map of Mexico on page 97 of *Activities for Communication* (Realia 5-1) or the map on page 156 of the *Pupil's Edition*. Each student should select three cities and write a complete weather report for each one. They should also list something they would like to do under those weather conditions.

Purpose to practice using vocabulary about the weather: talking about the weather and discussing things you like to do during each season

Rationale Doing research and then writing about it promotes critical thinking skills.

Materials No special materials are needed.

Portfolio Items Students may include their maps, weather reports and activities as part of their written portfolio.

Oral: Activity 30

Expanded Activity Have students prepare posters that depict their favorite season. The posters should be illustrated with different activities the student enjoys in that season. Illustrations may include photos, pictures from magazines, or drawings. Each one should have a caption. When the posters are finished, pairs of students interview each other about the posters: which season is depicted, why that season is the favorite, and how the illustrations show this. Each student asks questions, takes notes, and uses the notes to write a report about what the other student has said. Students then switch roles. Posters might be left up in the classroom for a week or so to stimulate conversation among the students.

Purpose to practice talking about seasonal activities and the weather: listening to people talk about how they spend their time, making notes of a conversation, and writing about it in the third person; discussing when and how often you do things and what you and your friends like to do together.

Rationale Students need to practice listening carefully, taking notes, and clarifying information.

Materials poster board, photos or pictures from magazines, paper, pen, pencil, audio or video recording equipment

Portfolio Item Record students interviewing each other while referring to the posters.

Entre familia

Written: Activity 37

Expanded Activity Students should think about their favorite TV family. Have them write at least six questions to ask their partner about the TV family. For example: What do the family members like to do? Where do they go on weekends? What household chores do they do? When the questionnaire is ready, students should ask two other students in the class about the lives of their chosen TV families.

Purpose to practice note-taking and making questions; to discuss things a family does together

Rationale Writing and talking about familiar topics will motivate students to use Spanish to communicate about their interests.

Materials No special materials are needed.

Portfolio Item A copy of the completed questionnaire can be added to the student's written portfolio.

Oral: Activity 22

Expanded Activity Have students write about what they'd like and not like to do on their birthday or some other special day. After students write about their day, have them get into groups and compare what they like and don't like to do. Each group should then agree on how to spend a day together.

Purpose to talk about activities one does with family and friends; describing a family, describing people, and discussing things a family does together

Rationale Putting daily activities into Spanish allows students frequent use of targeted language.

Material audio or video recording equipment (You may want to set the classroom up to resemble a TV studio with the name of the show written on or over the set—this could be a large table with chairs arranged in a U-shape. If the class is large, this activity can be done in two or more groups.)

Portfolio Item An audio or video recording of the mock TV show could be placed in each student's oral portfolio.

¿Qué te gustaría hacer?

Written: Activity 29

Expanded Activity Have students write a dialogue between themselves and their best friend. Suggested situation: Your friend has invited you to a birthday party but you have a more interesting suggestion. Decline the invitation to the birthday party and explain your plans. Be sure to make your plans sound irresistible and persuade him or her to come with you. Your best friend hesitates but finally accepts the invitation. Decide on a time and place to meet.

Purpose to practice vocabulary and functional expressions for making plans

Rationale This activity provides another opportunity to use the newly acquired target language in a real-life context.

Materials No special materials are needed.

Portfolio Item The revised composition can be placed in the student's written portfolio.

Oral: Activity 30

Expanded Activity Before students begin this activity, encourage them to write down phrases they think they'll need in order to decline and accept invitations. They should also review the vocabulary they'll need to talk on the phone. Tell students to think about one interesting thing they want to do over the weekend. Student 1 calls Student 2 on the phone and invites him or her to go out during the weekend. Student 2 declines the invitation, gives a polite excuse, and proposes something for the next weekend. Student 1 accepts the invitation. They agree on a time and place to meet.

Purpose to practice talking on the phone: extending and accepting invitations; making plans; turning down an invitation; and making an excuse

Rationale Talking on the phone is one of the most challenging communicative situations students will encounter. This activity gives them an opportunity to practice doing that and also to practice telephone courtesy.

Materials two phones, two chairs, video or audio recording equipment

Portfolio Item The final version of the telephone conversation can be recorded either on audio- or videocassette and can be added to the oral portfolio.

CAPÍTULO 8 — ¡A comer!

Written: Repaso Activity 3

Expanded Activity Divide your class into groups of three. Each group will prepare a restaurant menu from a different country. Have students look at the **Panorama cultural** and other culture notes in the chapter. They can also find information in cookbooks and on the Internet. Menus should include food by categories, the price, a short description of the dish, and the name of the restaurant. Encourage students to decorate their menus and be creative.

Purpose to practice food vocabulary; talking about meals and foods

Rationale One of the basic needs students will have if they visit a Spanish-speaking country is buying and ordering food. This activity will give them an opportunity to practice this vocabulary in an authentic context.

Materials markers, colored construction paper, pens, and glue sticks

Portfolio Item The completed menus can be placed in the student's written portfolio.

Oral: Activity 33

Expanded Activity Each group of three should pretend they're in a restaurant. They should bring props as needed, such as table decorations, napkins, tablecloths, salt and pepper shakers, and so on. Then, using the menus from the Written activity, have students play the roles of server and customers. (If students did not do the menu in the previous activity, have them turn to page 247 of the *Pupil's Edition* and use the menu in the text.) The customers ask for advice about different items on the menu. The server then serves the food. The customers make various comments about the food, and the server checks to make sure everything is all right. Finally, customers ask for the check, pay, and leave, bidding the server goodbye while she or he thanks them for their business.

Purpose to practice talking about meals and food: commenting on food; making polite requests; ordering dinner in a restaurant; asking for and paying the bill in a restaurant

Rationale Knowing restaurant etiquette and using correct language in a restaurant are essential skills.

Materials Students bring tables, chairs, menus and items for the table such as a tablecloth, silverware, and napkins, as well as decorations. Students may also want to use glasses with water and plates with some kind of food to simulate the dishes ordered, and video or audio recorder and player.

Portfolio Item The restaurant role-play can be recorded either on audio- or videocassette. The cassette can become part of the oral portfolio.

¡Vamos de compras!

Written: Activity 32

Expanded Activity Have students work with partners to create a page from a clothing catalog. Students can work with real catalogs, magazines, or their own drawings to illustrate wild or out-of-date styles. For example, they may choose a dress with stripes and plaid in orange and pink. Students should write a brief description of each item, including its color, style, material, size and cost. Encourage students to use their imagination and creativity in laying out the page. When the catalog page is complete, have students create an order form for the clothing items pictured.

Purpose to practice vocabulary about clothes, colors, styles, sizes, preferences, and appearance; to comment on clothes and asking about prices

Rationale Clothing is an important topic for most teens. An activity that enables them to use clothing vocabulary and expressions will be motivating to them.

Materials catalogs and magazines (for pictures), scissors, glue, felt-tipped pens, notebook or other paper for the order form, pens, and pencils

Portfolio Item The completed catalog page and order form can be added to the written portfolio.

Oral: Activity 31

Expanded Activity Pairs of students should use the catalog page they prepared in the Written Activity above, or else they should look on page 278 of the *Pupil's Edition* and prepare a catalog order form. One student role-plays the customer service representative of the catalog company. The representative has a blank order form. The other student plays a customer who calls by phone to order several items. The students playing the representative will give a negative opinion of each choice made by the customer, and suggest an alternative. The customer should agree to all new alternatives, even when they're uglier choices. After the customer has placed the order, students switch roles.

Purpose to practice discussing clothing items, colors, styles, sizes and cost; to practice talking on the phone; to comment on clothes and prices

Rationale Reinforcing vocabulary and functional expressions about clothes will be motivating to students. Knowing how to talk on the phone is a valuable skill for students to master.

Materials two telephones, catalog pages and order forms, audio or video recording equipment

Portfolio Item The recorded conversation (audio or visual) can be added to the oral portfolio.

Celebraciones

Written: Activity 38

Expanded Activity Have students think of all the things they would need to do to throw a successful party. Then have them imagine that a friend of theirs prepared everything for the last party they hosted. Students should write a paragraph describing at least 10 things the friend did to make their party a success.

Purpose to practice talking about past events and party vocabulary

Rationale Having students use the forms of the preterite in context will help them remember the forms more effectively.

Materials No special materials are needed.

Portfolio Item The finished composition can be placed in the student's written portfolio.

Oral: Repaso Activity 36

Expanded Activity Have students discuss in pairs what they did during the holidays mentioned on page 297 of the *Pupil's Edition*. They should think of at least two activities for each occasion. When the first student is done answering the questions, students should switch roles. For example: —¿**Qué hiciste el día del Padre?** —**Comí en casa de mi abuelo y compré un regalo para papá.**

Purpose to practice the preterite forms; to talk about holidays and special occasions

Rationale Students need to practice making and answering personal questions. This will help them recognize new vocabulary and verb forms.

Materials audio and video recording equipment

Portfolio Item A recording of the conversation can be placed in the student's oral portfolio.

Para vivir bien

Portfolio Suggestions

Written: Activity 31

Expanded Activity Students work individually using the pictures on p. 342 or other pictures the teacher may want to supply. The student chooses one picture and writes a story about that person's day. Students should use tenses for the past and present and then predict what the person is going to do after each action pictured. Students should name the person(s) in the picture and give a context: Who is in the picture? What is the activity? What prior events lead up to this moment? What is the time of day, the date, the season? How and why is this sequence of events taking place? Encourage students to describe the person(s) in the photo as fully and realistically as they can.

Purpose to practice using verb tenses, to use critical thinking skills of inference and predicting, to talk about moods and physical condition; saying what the person(s) in the photo did, where they went and when

Rationale In this activity students are given the opportunity to use their critical thinking skills in the target language and to integrate previously learned language skills with more recently learned ones. These two things will help them achieve proficiency.

Materials No special materials are needed.

Portfolio Item The finished story along with a copy of the pictures can be placed in the written portfolio.

Oral: Activity 19

Expanded Activity Pairs of students write various ailments on small slips of paper. There should be twelve slips of paper in all. The papers are folded and put in a hat to be drawn at random during the role-play. One student will play the doctor, the other the patient. The patient draws three ailments from the hat and pays a visit to the doctor to seek help with these problems. The students should greet each other as they would in a doctor's office. The doctor asks questions and the patient responds. The doctor should suggest a course of treatment for each problem, then the two say goodbye. The students then switch roles and a new set of ailments is drawn from the nine remaining in the hat. If the class is small and there is time, you may wish for students to use the remaining six slips of paper for a second visit to the doctor. Before recording the visit, they can then choose the three they prefer.

Purpose to practice using the present and past tense and to practice listening and responding: talking about physical conditions; making suggestions; expressing feelings; saying what you did

Rationale In this activity students practice listening to each other and exchanging real and meaningful information based on an authentic situation.

Materials paper and pens or pencils, classroom furniture arranged to simulate a doctor's office, video or audio recording equipment

Portfolio Item A recording (audio or video) of the role-play can become part of the oral portfolio.

Las vacaciones ideales

Written: Activity 34

Expanded Activity Have students imagine that they have just arrived at the place they've always dreamed of visiting! Students should prepare three picture postcards to send back to friends at home. They can draw pictures or use photos from magazines or travel brochures to prepare the postcards. On the other side of the card, students should write a note, using the present progressive tense, to report on what they are doing at that moment on their ideal vacation.

Purpose to practice appropriate vacation-related expressions and vocabulary; to talk about what you are doing on vacation

Rationale Students need to practice appropriate uses of verb tenses.

Materials 4 x 6-inch index cards, magazines or brochures, scissors, glue, felt-tipped pens, pen or pencil

Portfolio Item The three postcards can be added to the student's written portfolio.

Oral: Repaso Activity 3

Expanded Activity Pairs of students play a traveler and a travel agent. The traveler tells the agent in what kind of vacation he or she is interested as the agent takes notes. They then discuss possible destinations and talk about details, such as transportation, activities, and costs. When the traveler has made a final decision and they have made all of the arrangements (dates, times, tickets, hotels, activities), the travel agent should write an itinerary in a formal report and give it to the client. Students then exchange roles and repeat the process.

Purpose to practice verb tenses and vacation-related vocabulary; to talk about what you do and discuss what you would like to do on vacation

Rationale Students need to be able to express their personal preferences and wishes using the target language.

Materials posters and other visual aids to create a travel agency in the classroom, furniture arranged to simulate a travel office, audio or video recording equipment (Posters can be obtained from a travel agency or from an airline company. They could be created by the students themselves, perhaps in collaboration with the art teacher.)

Portfolio Item An audio or video recording of the conversation between the client and the travel agent can be placed in each student's oral portfolio.

Performance Assessment

¡Mucho gusto!

Performance Assessment

Primer paso

Hand pairs of students a three- to four-line situation written in English to practice one of the functional expressions learned in the **Primer paso**. For example: One student takes the role of Mr. Villanueva, and the other is the teenager, Gabriela. They will greet each other as if it were three in the afternoon. Allow students one minute to prepare and then act out the situation in Spanish. You can do this with small groups while other students are working on a separate activity.

Segundo paso

In small groups, have students create a situation (such as meeting a new exchange student or a famous person) in which they will introduce themselves and the chosen personality to each other and the class. Students need to introduce themselves by telling their name, their age, and where they are from (country or state). If time permits, set up a situation where students are entering a Spanish-speaking country and must pass through customs. The customs official asks for their names, ages, and countries of origin.

Tercer paso

In pairs, have students role-play the following situation. One is a famous sports figure, and the other a media interviewer. The interviewer asks the star questions related to his or her likes and dislikes (sports and food vocabulary). The star answers.

Global Assessment

Group students in pairs. Have one student be the new exchange student from Ecuador and the other be the person meeting him or her at the airport. When they role-play the scene with their partner, they should be sure to exchange names, ages, where they're from, and several likes and dislikes.

¡Organízate!

Primer paso

Bring ten school supplies that students carry in their **mochilas**. Ask students to copy the list of the items as you place them in the backpack. Then, as you pull an item out of the bag, call out a number (**uno** for the first item, **dos** for the second item, and so on). Ask students to write the number by the name of the item on their list.

Segundo paso

Divide students into groups of three. Assign or let students choose these roles: librarian, scribe, and proofreader. The librarian looks up words as needed, the scribe writes the description, and the proofreader checks for accuracy. Give each group a picture of a bedroom from a magazine. After discussing the things in the picture, each group writes a description of the room based on their discussion. All members of the group receive the same grade.

Tercer paso

Give each student a task to complete, written on a sheet of paper. (For example, you can assign them a chore like cleaning up their room.) Students should describe the steps that need to be accomplished to complete the task. This can be done on tape (video or audio) and presented in class. It can also be assigned to be written.

Global Assessment

Divide the class in groups of two or three. Have students imagine that they are from different Spanish-speaking countries, with new names and ages. They should introduce themselves to their group in Spanish and try to keep the conversation going as long as they can by asking their partners where they are from, what they have in their room, what they like and don't like, and what they want to do.

PERFORMANCE ASSESSMENT

Nuevas clases, nuevos amigos

Performance Assessment

Primer paso

In pairs, have students describe their schedules to each other as they would to a new friend. They should tell what classes they have at what time and indicate the order of their classes using **primero, después, luego,** and **por fin.** Have students present their dialogues to the class or record them on audio or videocassette.

Segundo paso

Make up an age-appropriate TV schedule and distribute the copies. Have students work in pairs to prepare a dialogue in which one student asks the times of various programs and the other student gives a response based on the TV schedule. Students could present their dialogues to the class or record them on an audio or videocassette.

Tercer paso

Give students a paper doll figure cut from poster board with no details. At the bottom of each figure leave room for a few sentences. Students decorate the figures as self-portraits with fabric, markers, etc. In the space they describe themselves using the sentences they wrote in Activity 34. You might have students present their self-portraits to classmates. The figures may be displayed in the classroom and saved to update with new information learned in later chapters.

Global Assessment

Have your students work with a partner. One of them will take the role of a reporter for the school newspaper. This student will interview Alejandro/a Morales, the new exchange student from Cuernavaca. The reporter will ask Alejandro/a questions about his classes, his schedule, and the things he likes and doesn't like. Students should take turns playing each role. One of the students will end the interview by saying he or she is late and in a hurry.

¿Qué haces esta tarde?

Primer paso

Have students describe the activities they prefer to do during their free time and those of their best friend. This could be done in writing or orally on audio- or videocassette.

Segundo paso

In groups, students develop and present a conversation in which they tell a new student where to find various persons and rooms in the school and some of their favorite places around town.

Tercer paso

In pairs, have students role-play the following situation: You're going to spend the weekend with a close friend in a neighboring town. Call a relative and let him or her know your plans. Your relative asks where you and your friend are going and what times you expect to be at each location. You should plan at least four activities during the weekend.

Global Assessment

Divide your class into groups of two or three students. Have them create a conversation in which they plan something fun to do. The problem is that everyone is busy! They should discuss their schedules and responsibilities and come to an agreement on the activity, the time, and the place where they'll meet.

CAPÍTULO 5
El ritmo de la vida

Performance Assessment

Primer paso

Ask students to write a letter in Spanish to a friend who is spending the year in Mexico. Ask them to include information about what some of her friends are doing this year, the day of the week on which they do it, or how often they do it. You may wish to show the students the Spanish style of using numbers for the date. (25/1/02=January 25, 2002). The letter might begin with **Querido/a** _____ and end with **Un saludo de** _____.

Segundo paso

Ask each student to make a daily planner for the coming weekend. Ask them to list the day of the week and use **por la mañana, por la tarde,** or **por la noche** with any activity they plan for that day.

Tercer paso

Ask pairs of students to role-play the following conversation. One is a cousin from a Spanish-speaking country in South America who is coming to visit the cousin in the United States and, in order to know what to bring, needs to know what the weather will be like and what they will be doing. (They may choose any season.) One cousin asks various questions, which the other student answers.

Global Assessment

With a partner, students will imagine they are hosting a late-night talk show. One student will be the host and the other a famous celebrity. The host should ask what their guest does during certain times of the year, what he or she likes to do on vacation, and where he or she likes to go and why.

PERFORMANCE ASSESSMENT

Entre familia

Primer paso

Ask students to develop a dialogue with a partner to present to the class. They are to pretend to be new acquaintances and ask each other about their families. They should demonstrate a real interest in each other's family with their questions. Answers should include descriptions of the family members. Remind students that their answers may be about an imaginary family.

Segundo paso

Ask students to develop a set of interview questions to find out about someone's family and what they like to do. You might set up your classroom like a TV talk show. Ask students to serve as host or hostess to interview someone in the class using their list of questions. Students should be sure to use questions and expressions from **Así se dice** on pages 178 and 180 of the *Pupil's Edition.*

Tercer paso

Ask students to create a note to a younger brother or sister, listing at least five chores that need to be done on a Saturday.

Global Assessment

Have your students role-play the following situations with a partner:

a. Partner A has just arrived at his or her host family's house in Bolivia. Partner B introduces the family and then asks about the partner's family. Partner A should describe each family member and what his or her family likes to do together.

b. A student is going to have a party at her or his house on Saturday night. Five friends volunteer to help get the house ready for the party. The student should tell each friend what they need to do.

¿Qué te gustaría hacer?

Performance Assessment

Primer paso

Working in pairs, have students role-play Activity 14, part 2. They should incorporate at least three verbs and three new vocabulary words. Have students role-play the phone conversation for the rest of the class. You may choose to record this for an oral Portfolio entry or grade it as students perform. You may wish to allow some students to write the dialogue instead of acting it out.

Segundo paso

Ask students to work with a partner. Each pair is to create a party invitation that contains all the usual information: host, honoree, occasion, time, and place. Encourage them to embellish the invitation with activities planned, to indicate if it's a surprise party, and to give suggestions on what to bring. Have partners decorate the invitations and post them on a class bulletin board. You might consider having students send their invitations to another Spanish class.

Tercer paso

Group Work Divide the class into "families" of three or four. Ask each family to role-play a dialogue among family members. They should ask each other to do various things around the house. In response, each is to decline, refuse, or accept what they are asked to do. Each family member should interact with at least two others. You might have groups present their conversations to the class. You could record the dialogues and put them in student Portfolios if appropriate.

Global Assessment

Have students imagine that their Great-Aunt Hortensia has invited them to an accordion concert (**concierto de acordeón**) this Saturday. They already have plans to go out with their friends, but they do not want to hurt her feelings. With a classmate, have students take turns role-playing a conversation between them and their **tía abuela** Hortensia. They should politely turn down her invitation and explain why, remembering to thank her for the invitation.

¡A comer!

Primer paso

Have students make a shopping list of foods to buy for a week of breakfasts and lunches. They should then make a meal calendar for the week and describe to the class what they plan to eat at each meal. Encourage students to consider whether or not they are choosing healthy foods.

Segundo paso

Have students discuss their restaurant review from Activity 25. They should include a description of the establishment (diner, elegant restaurant, fast-food place) and what it serves (breakfast foods, lunch specials). As each student discusses their restaurant with their partners, encourage them to ask questions about the food, the atmosphere and the specials.

Tercer paso

Use a modification of Activity 35 for performance assessment. Every time the customer asks for something, the server says they do not have it, and offers to bring the customer something else. The customer should ask for five different items, and the server should come up with five different alternatives. Students should present their conversation to the class.

Global Assessment

Have students work in groups of three to create an original scene for one of the following situations. Have them role-play their scene for the class.

a. You and a friend have just finished eating lunch. The waitperson asks you if you want anything else and suggests a dessert. You politely decline and ask for the check. The waitperson tells you how much you owe. You pay the check and leave a tip.

b. You and your family are out for a nice dinner, but everything is going wrong! The waitperson forgets to give you the menu, the silverware is dirty, and when the food comes, it's cold and doesn't taste good. Point out the problems and politely request the things you need. Be creative, but mind your manners!

¡Vamos de compras!

Primer paso

Ask students to write a note in Spanish to their parent or guardian saying that they are not going to be home right after school because they have to buy a gift for a friend. They should include what they plan to give the friend and where they are going to buy the gift.

Segundo paso

Have students write a letter to a friend describing their favorite outfit. They should include colors, fabrics, information about where they wear it, and a comparison of this outfit with others.

Tercer paso

Pairs of students create a dialogue between a customer and the clerk in a clothing store. Have them include expressions of courtesy, express preferences, inquire about prices, and pay. The work may be performed or written. Encourage students to try out different selling styles (hard sell, soft sell).

Global Assessment

Ask students to create a store within the classroom. They should gather materials to "sell," choose clerks, make signs and price tags, and set up a cashier's station. Then, have them use the vocabulary and grammar from this chapter to "buy and sell" the merchandise.

Celebraciones

Primer paso

Have students describe how your school celebrates one of the holidays on page 297 or how your class celebrates another special event. Ask them to imagine it is one of these days and ask them what people are doing to prepare for the party. Ask them to name some special activities that take place during one of the holidays. Are there any special celebrations or parties related to that day? Students should come up with a list of special activities that take place during that time of the year.

Segundo paso

Tell students that a family is planning a big party for the grandparents' wedding anniversary. The person in charge of planning the party has errands to run and cannot direct preparations. Ask students to write a list telling each member of the family what he or she is to do to help prepare for the party. They may include any number of people in the family for this activity.

Tercer paso

Have students work in pairs to role-play a telephone conversation in which they talk about what they did this past weekend. Students should be prepared to present their dialogue to the class.

Global Assessment

Have students imagine that they are part of a committee to plan the end-of-the-year dance. There is a problem. The class doesn't have enough money. Working in groups of three or four, students should discuss a solution to the problem. They should give their opinion about food, activities, and a location that will fit their budget. They should also suggest ways to earn money for the project and should, finally, present their ideas to the class.

Para vivir bien

Primer paso

Type the following letter on a handout for students or write it on the board or on a transparency. Then, have students write a response to Pedro.

Querido/a_____,
Vas a llegar para tu visita a Puerto Rico en menos de dos semanas. Tengo muchas ganas de verte y salir a conocer la isla. Estoy haciendo planes interesantes y vamos a pasarlo muy bien. ¿Qué tal si todas las mañanas vamos al gimnasio a las seis para levantar pesas y hacer ejercicio? También podemos bucear y luego mirar la televisión por un par de horas. Escríbeme una carta para decirme las cosas que te gustaría hacer. Hasta pronto.
Tu primo, Pedro

Segundo paso

Ask students to write a dialogue between a doctor and patient using as much of the vocabulary as possible from this **paso**. The patient should complain about two or three things, and the doctor should offer advice. When they have completed their dialogues, have students present them to the class. You might grade both the written dialogues and oral presentations.

Tercer paso

Ask students to write a summary of a recent memorable trip or weekend. Have them write five sentences saying what they did, where they went, and when. You might have them present their sentences to the class. Remind them that they may include imaginary information.

Global Assessment

In groups of three or four, students should invite each other to go to a variety of places in San Juan. They should turn down some invitations and make suggestions of other places to go. In the end, they decide on an activity and present the scene to the class.

12 Las vacaciones ideales

Performance Assessment

Primer paso

Have students write a letter to a travel agent requesting information on a place they plan to visit. Each student should ask the cost of the ticket, when the plane will leave, and what he or she will need to take.

Segundo paso

Students in pairs create a dialogue between a travel agent and a client using as much of the vocabulary as possible from this **Paso**. When they have completed their dialogues, students present them to the class. If possible, have props available, such as used airline tickets, a passport, or an itinerary. See *Activities for Communication*, Realia 1-2 (page 76) for a passport application form. Consider grading both the written dialogues and oral presentations.

Tercer paso

Ask students to imagine they have just returned from a vacation. They are to create a photo album with pictures clipped from magazines and write a brief description under each picture explaining where they were and what they were doing or seeing when the photo was taken.

Global Assessment

Have your students imagine they are on a bus from San Juan to Ponce and they strike up a conversation with the person next to them. With a partner, they can role-play a scene where they find out their fellow passenger's name and age and where he or she is from. They should also ask where their new friend is going, what he or she plans to do there, where their friend went in Puerto Rico, and what he or she did there. Students need to switch roles and be prepared to present the scene to the class.

PERFORMANCE ASSESSMENT

Using CD-ROM for Assessment

¡Mucho gusto!

DISC 1

Guided Recording

¡A hablar!
Students record a conversation with a partner based on the following prompts:

STUDENT A Say hello and tell your partner your name.
STUDENT B Say your name and that you're glad to meet him or her. Ask how your partner is doing.
STUDENT A Say you're feeling okay and ask your partner how he or she is feeling.
STUDENT B Say you're feeling great. Then ask your partner where he or she is from.
STUDENT A Tell where you're from. Tell your partner you have to go and will see him or her later.
STUDENT B Tell your partner good-bye.

Have students make note of words and expressions they plan to use in **¡A hablar!**

Guided Writing

¡A escribir!
Students choose from among the following writing scenarios:

 List A friend of yours who doesn't know Spanish is going to Spain on vacation. Create a sheet for him or her with three ways to greet someone and three ways to say good-bye.

 Letter A pen pal organization has offered to forward a letter from you to a student in Spain. Write a short message telling your name and where you're from, and asking this person's name and where he or she is from.

 Questionnaire You're creating a questionnaire for a school pen pal program. Write three questions to be answered by someone trying to find a pen pal.

 Questionnaire Answer the questions on the questionnaire above.

Para hispanohablantes

Imagina que hay un nuevo estudiante de intercambio en tu escuela. Escribe una conversación entre tú y esta persona. Primero preséntate y pregúntale cómo está. Luego pregúntale de dónde es y menciona de dónde eres. Después discutan ustedes algunas de las cosas que les gustan y que no les gustan. Por fin, presenta al nuevo estudiante a uno de tus amigos.

Encourage students to use the online resources, such as the Vocabulary ("V") and the Grammar Summary ("G"), when completing their assignments. These resources may be accessed from the control panel at the bottom of their screen. Some students may also want to refer to their textbook.

¡Organízate!

Guided Recording

¡A hablar!

Students record a conversation by responding to the following prompts:

1. ¿Necesitas una mochila?
2. ¿Cuántas carpetas necesitas?
3. ¿Cuántas plumas necesita tu hermana?
4. ¿Qué más necesitas para la escuela?
5. Y ¿qué más necesita tu hermana?
6. ¿Qué quieres para tu cuarto?

To aid students with visual and kinesthetic learning styles, have students write their answers to the **¡A hablar!** prompts before recording them.

Guided Writing

¡A escribir!

Students choose from among the following writing scenarios:

 List Imagine you're getting ready for the beginning of school. Write a list of the things you want and need to do before school starts.

 Description Your family is moving into a new house. The moving company wants to know how much space they'll need for your things in their van. Help them by describing the contents of your room.

 Conversation Your mother has asked you to take your younger brother or sister shopping for school supplies. Ask a partner to play the role of your brother or sister and create a conversation in which you talk about what he or she needs for school.

 Script You and a friend are planning to spend some time together this Saturday. Both of you have errands to run, but you'll also have time for other things. With a partner, write a skit in which you discuss what you each need and want to do on Saturday.

(Para hispanohablantes)

Imagina que hoy es el 20 de agosto y que las clases empiezan el 24 de agosto. Escribe una lista de cuatro cosas que tienes que hacer y tres cosas que quieres hacer antes del 24 de agosto.

Have students who write the conversation or the script record it with a partner.

You might have students who write the description above elaborate on it. Ask them to imagine that their bedroom in their family's new home is much larger than their current room. Ask them to describe what they want to have in their new space.

Nuevas clases, nuevos amigos

Guided Recording

¡A hablar!
Students record a conversation with a partner based on the following prompts:

STUDENT A Ask your friend what classes he or she has this semester.

STUDENT B Say that you have math, computer programming, physical education, geography, and Spanish.

STUDENT A Ask your friend what time his or her computer programming class is.

STUDENT B Respond that your computer programming class is at 8:15.

STUDENT A Ask your friend what his or her favorite teacher is like.

STUDENT B Say that he or she is intelligent, interesting, nice, and fun.

Guided Writing

¡A escribir!
Students choose from among the following writing scenarios:

 Letter Write a letter telling a friend about the classes you're taking this semester and when you have each one. Close by saying you have to go because you're late for class.

 Article Write an article about your favorite class for the school newspaper. In six or seven sentences, say which class you like the most and why.

 Note A friend of yours has just moved to your community and wants to know what people at your school are like. Write him or her a note in which you describe some of your friends and teachers.

 E-mail Write an e-mail to a student who plans to attend your school next semester. Be sure to describe what the classes at your school are like.

(**Para hispanohablantes**)

Con un compañero, escribe una conversación en que hablen de las clases que un amigo toma. Menciona a qué hora tiene cada clase, qué clases le gustan o no le gustan, y por qué.

CAPÍTULO **4** DISC 1

¿Qué haces esta tarde?

CD-ROM Assessment

Guided Recording

¡A hablar!
Students record a conversation with a partner based on the following prompts:

STUDENT A Ask your partner what he or she likes to do after school.

STUDENT B Answer by saying that you go to the park to listen to music.

STUDENT A Ask where the park is.

STUDENT B Say that the park is near your school.

STUDENT A Ask your partner if he or she likes to practice sports during free time.

STUDENT B Say that you like to ride your bike and play tennis.

 Have students write some useful words and expressions before recording the **¡A hablar!** conversation. Encourage them to use brief notes rather than reading a script word for word.

Guided Writing

¡A escribir!
Students choose from among the following writing scenarios:

 E-mail Imagine you're getting to know a Mexican student through e-mail. Write a letter about what you like to do during your free time and ask what the student and his or her family like to do during their free time.

 Brochure Imagine you're writing a brochure about your community for the local chamber of commerce. Write a paragraph about several interesting places in your community, where these places are, and what people do at each place.

 Article Write a feature article for the school newspaper in which you interview several students at your school about what they do in their free time and who they spend it with.

 Letter Imagine that a relative in another state or country wants to know more about what you do during your free time. Write him or her a note about where you go and what you do each day of the week when you have free time.

(Para hispanohablantes)

En tres o cuatro párrafos, escribe una descripción para el periódico de un club de recreo. No te olvides de mencionar dónde y cuándo tiene lugar cada actividad.

CD-ROM ASSESSMENT

¡Ven conmigo! Level 1

Alternative Assessment Guide **49**

CAPÍTULO

DISC 2

El ritmo de la vida

CD-ROM Assessment

Guided Recording

¡A hablar!

Students record a conversation with a partner based on the following prompts:

1. ¡Hola! ¿Qué tiempo hace hoy?
2. Oye, a mí me gusta mucho el tenis. ¿Con qué frecuencia juegas al tenis?
3. Yo estudio con mis amigos y amigas todos los días. ¿Y tú?
4. Y ¿qué haces durante la semana?
5. ¿Qué te gusta hacer los fines de semana?

Guided Writing

¡A escribir!

Students choose from among the following writing scenarios:

Article Imagine you're the society reporter for a major newspaper. Write an interview in which you ask a famous person about his or her pastimes and how often he or she participates in each one. Be sure to include the famous person's responses.

E-mail Imagine that you and a student in another state are corresponding through the Internet. Write an e-mail message telling what you do in a typical week. Also ask what he or she does in a typical week.

Letter Write a letter to a relative in which you talk about what you and your friends like to do for fun. Include a few activities that everyone in the group likes, and some that only a few people like.

Script Imagine you're writing a script for tonight's TV weather report. Begin by giving today's date. Then tell what the weather is like today in your community and in other parts of the country. Indicate if this weather is typical of the season.

Para hispanohablantes

Escribe lo que les gusta hacer a ti y a tus amigos durante una semana típica en cada una de las cuatro estaciones. Cuando sea posible, menciona por qué la actividad es apropiada para la estación. Tu párrafo debe ser de unas 12 frases.

CD-ROM ASSESSMENT

CAPÍTULO 6
DISC 2

Entre familia

Guided Recording

¡A hablar!

Students record a conversation with a partner based on the following prompts:

STUDENT A Ask how many people are in your partner's family.

STUDENT B Respond that there are five of you, and ask how many are in your partner's family.

STUDENT A Say that there are four people in your family. Ask how many brothers and sisters your partner has.

STUDENT B Respond that you have an older brother and a younger sister.

STUDENT A Ask what your partner's brother and sister are like.

STUDENT B Say that your brother is slender, red-headed, and has blue eyes, and that your sister is mischievous but very affectionate.

Guided Writing

¡A escribir!

Students choose from among the following writing scenarios. The first activity emphasizes the writing process.

 Article Write a magazine article of 8–10 sentences describing a fictitious sports or entertainment figure and his or her family.

 Conversation Write a conversation of about 10 lines in which your best friend tells you about a problem and you give some advice.

 Questionnaire Imagine that you're conducting a survey about other students' families. Write a questionnaire of 6–8 questions you would ask.

 Creative Writing In 10–15 sentences, write a story about your family for a home-made family history book. Be sure to identify the members of your family, describe them briefly, and mention some things that your family does together.

(Para hispanohablantes)

Imagina que escribes un párrafo para tu diario. Tú y tus familiares se han puesto de acuerdo sobre los quehaceres domésticos. Haz una lista de los quehaceres que tú y los demás van a hacer en el futuro. Luego escribe un párrafo de 10–15 frases sobre las actividades de la familia.

Have students use the following steps to complete their articles:

PREWRITING Think of a fictitious celebrity you'd like to write about. Then make a list of adjectives that describe the celebrity and his or her family members.

WRITING Write a short paragraph about the celebrity and his or her family, using the adjectives you created in your PREWRITING list. You may also include any other appropriate adjectives that come to mind.

REVISING Print out your article, make any necessary changes to improve it, and check it for correct spelling, accents, and capitalization.

PUBLISHING Correct any errors, and print out a copy of your finished article. You may wish to add illustrations to your article.

CD-ROM ASSESSMENT

¿Qué te gustaría hacer?

Guided Recording

¡A hablar!

Students record a conversation by responding to the following prompts:

1. ¡Hola! Vamos al cine en una hora, ¿no? Yo estoy listo... ¿y tú?
2. ¿Te gustaría ir a un café después de la película? Te invito...
3. Oye, ¿qué planes tienes para mañana?
4. ¿Tienes tiempo para ir al zoológico mañana?
5. Y quiero ir al circo en dos semanas. ¿Te gustaría ir?

Guided Writing

¡A escribir!

Students choose from among the following writing scenarios:

 Dialogue Write a dialogue in which you call a place of business and ask for a friend who works there. The secretary asks who's calling and you respond. The secretary then tells you your friend's line is busy. You thank the secretary and say you'll call back later.

 E-mail Imagine a friend wrote you an e-mail to ask if you're ready to go to a birthday party you've both been invited to. Write your friend an e-mail reply in which you say what you need to do to get ready.

 Letter Write a letter to a friend in which you talk about several places you're planning to visit on your vacation next week. Don't forget to mention things you're going to do at each place.

 Script Write a script in which a good friend invites you to go several places. Each time, you respond that you can't, and explain why.

Para hispanohablantes

Escribe el guión para una conversación entre una pareja en una telenovela. El hombre le pregunta a la mujer si está lista para ir al teatro. La mujer le dice lo que tiene que hacer antes de ir al teatro. Luego el hombre le pregunta si quiere ir al circo mañana. Ella le dice que no y explica por qué.

CAPÍTULO **8**

DISC 2

¡A comer!

CD-ROM Assessment

Guided Recording

¡A hablar!

Students record a conversation based on the following prompts:

STUDENT A Say what you usually eat here, and ask what your partner usually has.

STUDENT B Say what you usually eat and what you plan to order. Then ask what your partner plans to order.

STUDENT A Say what you plan to order today.

STUDENT B Say how your food is, and ask how your partner's food is.

STUDENT A Tell your partner how your food is. Then ask how much the bill is and if the tip is included.

STUDENT B Say how much the bill is and whether the tip is included.

> You might have students review the functional phrases for ordering dinner and asking for and paying the bill in a restaurant on page 246 of the *Pupil's Edition* before recording the ¡A hablar! activity.

Guided Writing

¡A escribir!

Students choose from among the following writing scenarios:

 Menu Create a menu for a restaurant that you would like to own someday. Be sure to include all three meals and create some combination specials. Don't forget to include prices and a name for your restaurant!

 Review Imagine you're a food critic for a local newspaper. Write a description of a restaurant in your community where you've dined recently. Describe the food, service, and prices.

 Script Write a script about two friends eating at a restaurant. One of them loves the food and the other doesn't. Have them discuss the food and explain their likes and dislikes.

 Dialogue Imagine you're having dinner with your grandparents at their favorite restaurant. Write a dialogue in which you discuss what each of you wants to eat. Finish the dialogue by placing your orders.

(Para hispanohablantes)

Escribe un artículo sobre un nuevo restaurante ecuatoriano en tu ciudad. Menciona algunas de las comidas típicas del Ecuador, los precios y la calidad de servicio.

CD-ROM ASSESSMENT

¡Ven conmigo! Level 1

Alternative Assessment Guide **53**

¡Vamos de compras!

Guided Recording

¡A hablar!

Students record a conversation with a partner based on the following prompts:

STUDENT A Ask the customer what kind of gift he or she is looking for.

STUDENT B Tell the salesperson that you're looking for a leather jacket for a friend.

STUDENT A Tell the customer you have a blue jacket and a black jacket.

STUDENT B Ask the salesperson how much each jacket costs.

STUDENT A Tell the customer that the blue jacket is more expensive than the black one. Ask the customer which one he or she prefers.

STUDENT B Tell the salesperson you prefer the black one.

Guided Writing

¡A escribir!

Students choose from among the following writing scenarios:

 Conversation Imagine tomorrow is your best friend's birthday. Write a conversation in which you tell a clothing salesperson what kind of gift you're looking for and the salesperson tells you what he or she has in stock. Then ask the salesperson how much these items cost.

 Dialogue Imagine you're vacationing in a large city in Latin America. You'd like to go to a bakery, a candy shop, and a florist. Write a conversation in which you ask a local resident how to find these places.

 Advertisement Imagine you're the marketing director for a large clothing store. Write a newspaper advertisement that describes five or six items you have on sale this week. Be sure to give your clothing store a creative name.

 E-mail Imagine you and a friend are sharing the cost of a gift for your favorite teacher. Write your friend an e-mail describing two or three gift possibilities. Mention that one of the gifts is more (or less) expensive than the others. Then indicate which gift you think you and your friend should buy and why.

Para hispanohablantes

Escribe una conversación en la cual tú le preguntes a un amigo qué debes comprar para el cumpleaños de tu prima favorita. Luego le preguntas a tu amigo dónde debes comprar este regalo y cómo se llega a la tienda apropiada. Luego pregunta qué ropa debes llevar a la fiesta de cumpleaños.

Guided Recording

¡A hablar!
Students record a conversation based on the following prompts.
1. Bueno, sabes que hoy es el cumpleaños de mi hermana. ¿Me ayudas a decorar la casa para la fiesta?
2. ¿Me haces el favor de llamar a los invitados?
3. ¿Qué te parece si escuchamos unos discos compactos durante la fiesta?
4. Compré un collar para mi hermana. ¿Qué compraste tú para ella?
5. ¿Crees que hay bastante comida para la fiesta?

Guided Writing

¡A escribir!
Students choose from among the following writing scenarios.

 E-mail Imagine that you're at your birthday party. Write an e-mail telling your Spanish-speaking pen pal that you're at your birthday party and telling him or her what you and your friends are doing at the party.

 "How-to" Instructions Imagine that you're planning a celebration at your school. Write a list of instructions telling several of your friends what to do to help.

 Dialogue Write a dialogue in which you ask your friend's opinion about what specific things to do to prepare for a party you're giving. Your friend indicates whether he or she thinks each idea is a good one.

 Movie script Write a short movie scene in which a teen girl asks a teen boy why he didn't come to her birthday party the day before yesterday. He apologizes and explains where he went and what he did.

Para hispanohablantes

Imagina que tú y una amiga están haciendo los preparativos para una fiesta de Año Nuevo. Ustedes hablan de lo que hicieron anoche y tú le dices tres o cuatro cosas que ella puede hacer para ayudarte. Escribe la conversación.

 Have pairs of students work together on any one of the writing assignments above. Encourage them to review each other's work and give constructive criticism. Students should save drafts of their written work, but should turn in a version that includes peer edits.

CD-ROM ASSESSMENT

Para vivir bien

Guided Recording

¡A hablar!
Students record a conversation based on the following prompts.

STUDENT A Ask if your partner wants to go roller skating at 7:00 P.M.

STUDENT B Respond that you don't feel like it today.

STUDENT A Ask your partner why and ask how he or she is feeling today.

STUDENT B Respond that you have a cold. Mention that your friend Ramón also isn't feeling well.

STUDENT A Ask your partner what's wrong with Ramón.

STUDENT B Tell your partner that Ramón went home and that you think he has the flu.

Guided Writing

¡A escribir!
Students choose from among the following writing scenarios.

 Dialogue Write a conversation in which you ask if a friend would like to lift weights with you. Your friend responds that he or she doesn't feel like it. You ask what's wrong, and your partner says he or she has the flu.

 Note Write a note to a friend asking what she or he did last night. Tell your friend that you studied in the library and then you and some friends played soccer. Mention that you didn't win, and close by inviting your friend to go to a concert tonight.

 Letter Imagine you and your family just got back from an extended vacation. Write a letter to a relative telling all the places you and other members of your family went.

 Journal Imagine you're a famous professional tennis player. Compose a journal entry about things you did this week. Tell where you went and the players and celebrities you played tennis with, and indicate whether or not you won.

(Para hispanohablantes)

Imagina que tienes una amiga que parece estar un poco preocupada. Escribe una conversación en la que tú le preguntas qué tiene. Tu amiga responde que jugó al baloncesto por cinco horas anoche y que ahora tiene tos y le duele la cabeza. Pregúntale a tu amiga por qué no va a casa para descansar. Tu amiga te agradece el consejo y dice que va a regresar a casa ahora mismo.

CD-ROM ASSESSMENT

Las vacaciones ideales

Guided Recording

¡A hablar!
Students record a conversation based on the following prompts.

STUDENT A Ask what your partner plans to do this summer.

STUDENT B Say that you intend to travel to Puerto Rico.

STUDENT A Say that you think your partner traveled to Puerto Rico last year.

STUDENT B Tell your partner you did go to Puerto Rico last year but would like to go this year also.

STUDENT A Ask what your partner would like to do in Puerto Rico this year.

STUDENT B Say that you hope to visit Ponce first and that you'd like to go to San Juan afterwards.

Guided Writing

¡A escribir!
Students choose from among the following four writing scenarios. The first activity emphasizes the writing process.

 Letter Write a letter telling a friend about the dream vacation you're planning.

 Conversation Write a conversation of 8–10 lines in which you ask a friend about his or her vacation plans. Your friend tells you about the vacation he or she would like to take this summer and the things he or she wants to do.

 Postcard Imagine you're vacationing in an exotic place. Write a postcard to a friend about three places you went yesterday and what you did at each place.

 Questionnaire Write a 6–8 item questionnaire that you could use to interview people about previous vacations and vacations they would like to take.

Para hispanohablantes

Imagina que escribes una columna mensual sobre viajes y vacaciones para el periódico de tu comunidad. En tu trabajo tienes que visitar muchos locales turísticos y escribir artículos sobre ellos. Escribe un artículo de 15 frases sobre el lugar que visitaste el mes pasado y lo que hiciste allí. Entonces menciona el lugar que te gustaría visitar el mes que viene y explica por qué te interesa.

Have students use the following steps to complete their letters.

PREWRITING Make a list of three or four places you'd like to visit on your dream vacation, and quickly jot down several things you'd like to see and do at each place.

WRITING Choose a destination from your PREWRITING list. Then write a brief letter listing, in order, the things you'd like to see and do.

REVISING Print your letter, make any necessary changes to improve it, and check it for correct spelling, accents, and capitalization.

PUBLISHING Correct any errors and print a copy of your finished letter. You may wish to add illustrations to your letter and share it with your classmates.